LIBRARY
LONGFELLOW ELEMENTARY SCHOOL

JEWISH
FOOD AND DRINK

Aviva Paraïso

The Bookwright Press
New York · 1989

FOOD AND DRINK

African Food and Drink
Australasian Food and Drink
British Food and Drink
Caribbean Food and Drink
Chinese Food and Drink
French Food and Drink
Greek Food and Drink
Indian Food and Drink
Italian Food and Drink

Japanese Food and Drink
Jewish Food and Drink
Mexican Food and Drink
Middle Eastern Food and Drink
North American Food and Drink
Russian Food and Drink
Southeast Asian Food and Drink
Spanish Food and Drink
West German Food and Drink

First published in the
United States in 1989 by
The Bookwright Press
387 Park Avenue South
New York, NY 10016

First published in 1988 by
Wayland (Publishers) Limited
61 Western Road, Hove
East Sussex BN3 1JD, England

© Copyright 1988 Wayland (Publishers) Limited
All rights reserved

Library of Congress Cataloging-in-Publication Data

Paraiso, Aviva
  Jewish food and drink / by Aviva Paraiso
    p. cm. — (Food and drink)
  Bibliography: p.
  Includes index.
  Summary: Describes, in text and illustrations, the food and beverages of the Jewish people in relation to their history, geography, and culture. Includes recipes.
    ISBN 0–531–18233–9
    1. Cookery, Jewish—Juvenile literature.
2. Beverages—Juvenile literature.
[1. Cookery, Jewish. 2. Jews—Social life and customs.]   I. Title.   II. Series.
TX724.P37 1989
394.1'089924–dc19   88–26230
                                       CIP
                                        AC

Typeset by DP Press, Sevenoaks
Printed in Italy by G. Canale & C.S.p.A., Turin

Contents

The countries and the people	4
The history of Jewish food	9
Food production	18
Processing and selling the food	23
Food and health	27
Cooking Shabbat meals	29
Drinks	33
Festive foods	35
Appendix	44
Glossary	44
Further reading	46
Index	47

The countries and the people

The Jewish people believe that God gave them the land of Israel as their own for all time. In 1948, this dream came true when the modern State of Israel came into existence.

Israel is surrounded by Lebanon to the north, Syria and Jordan to the east, Egypt to the southwest, and the Mediterranean Sea to the west. Israel covers an area of 20,323 sq km (7,847 sq mi) and has a population of around 4 million.

Below *Parts of Israel are very fertile. This picture was taken near where the Jordan River joins the Sea of Galilee.*

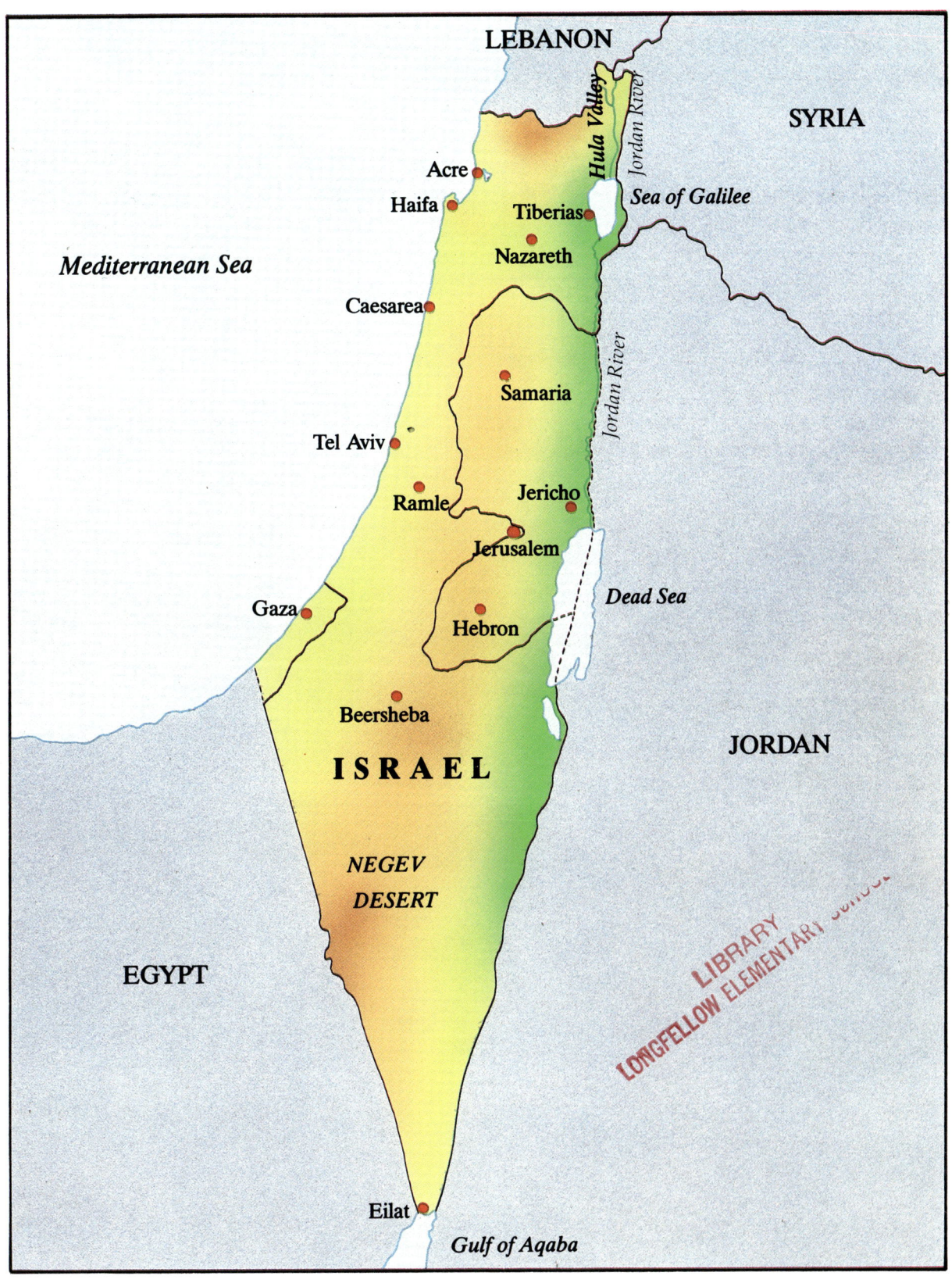

Millions more Jews are spread throughout the world. There are over six million Jews in the United States alone; others live in Australia, Canada, Europe, the USSR and Poland. These Jewish communities outside Israel are known as the Diaspora.

The Jews have a long and complicated history. For centuries they have been persecuted. Only since 1948 have they had a land they can call their own. But even now, they feel threatened by the Arab nations.

Their story begins in the year 2000 BC in the city of Ur in Mesopotamia, now Iraq. According to the Bible, a man called Abraham, who lived in Ur, turned away from the many nature-gods of his people and worshiped one god who was known as Yahweh, or Jahveh. Abraham made an agreement with this god that he and his family would always worship him. Jahveh promised that he would look after Abraham's descendants.

This Jewish food store is in the city of Istanbul in Turkey. Jews have lived in the city since the thirteenth century.

This family of Sephardic Jews, perhaps originally from North Africa, Spain or Portugal, are celebrating Passover in Jerusalem.

The citizens of Ur and of the neighboring cities traded with the cities of Canaan on the coast of the Mediterranean Sea. As trade increased, whole families moved to Canaan and took the religion of Abraham with them.

When Canaan was hit by famine, many people traveled to the land of their Egyptian trading partners to live, where they were forced into slavery by the Egyptians. Finally, in about 1250 BC, they fled from their oppressors under the leadership of Moses. The Jews lived in the wilderness for forty years until Moses' successor, Joshua, eventually led the Jews back to Canaan. They became a nation called the Israelites.

Later, under attack from the Philistines, they chose a king to lead them. Their first king, David, unified the nation of Israel and began to build a city near the present site of Jerusalem. David's son, Solomon, built a great temple in Jerusalem to house the Ark of the Covenant, in which were kept the Ten Commandments given to Moses in the wilderness.

In 920 BC, the kingdom split. In the north was Israel with a new capital at Samaria and in the south, Judah with its capital, Jerusalem.

The Assyrians conquered Israel in 722 BC, and many Jews fled to Persia. Judah was conquered by the Babylonians, and the Temple was destroyed in 586 BC. Many Jews were carried off in captivity to Babylonia. Their desire to return to their homeland was granted when Cyrus the Persian conquered the Babylonians and ordered the rebuilding of the Temple. Many Israelites returned to their country, now called Palestine. However, others remained in Babylonia and built up an important Jewish center. By this time there were also large Jewish communities in Egypt, Syria and Persia.

In the first century BC, the Romans moved into Palestine. Once again, many Jews fled, settling as far afield as Spain, France and, later, England and Germany. Persecution in Germany forced them into Poland and Russia. Those who settled in northern, central and eastern Europe were known as Ashkenazi; those who settled in Spain, Portugal and North Africa were called Sephardi.

The Sephardic Jews found themselves under Muslim rule and prospered, rising to positions of power in the tenth and eleventh centuries AD.

Since the thirteenth century, the history of the Jews is one of persecution and expulsion from countries in which they have settled. By the seventeenth century, there were Jewish communities in many cities of western Europe. There was tolerance rather than acceptance; however, by the 1880s, strong anti-Semite movements were developing in Germany and France. Also at this time, many Jews were driven out of western Russia and went to Europe and North America.

During the World War II, 1939–45, six million Jews were killed in the German concentration camps. This was a third of the world's total Jewish population.

The creation of the State of Israel in 1948 saw many Jews from all over the Diaspora return to live in their historical homeland.

The history of Jewish food

The food laws of the Jewish people are a vital part of their religion and form a constant link with the past and reminder of their history. The books of Leviticus (Chapter 11) and Deuteronomy (Chapter 14) in the Old Testament of the Bible give various food laws that are still strictly adhered to by many Jews today.

Practicing Jews are allowed to eat only *kosher* food. *Kosher* means "permitted." They may not eat food that is *terefah* (forbidden).

Jews may eat the meat or meat

These chickens are on sale in a poultry market in west Jerusalem. You can see that the butcher is wearing a special apron called a kapel.

products of animals that have cloven hoofs and chew their cud, when they have been slaughtered by a ritual method, known as *shechitah*. This excludes pork. Only the fore-quarters of animals are *kosher*.

Fish with scales, fins and a backbone are permitted, but shellfish are not. Certain types of birds such as chickens are also allowed if they are slaughtered correctly.

Meat and dairy products must not be eaten or cooked together, as it says in the Bible, "Thou shalt not seethe [boil] a kid in its mother's milk" (Deuteronomy, Chapter 14).

There are three different types of food: meat, milk and *parve* (or *parev*). Meat covers all *kosher* meat and meat products. Milk includes all milk and milk products – hard cheese made with animal rennet is not permitted. *Parve* are all foods that are not meat or milk, such as eggs (these must be checked for bloodspots before using), vegetables, fruits, cereals, beans and pulses and fish. Honey is also included in this group. Bees are not *kosher*, but the argument is that the honey is never actually part of the bee, only carried by it.

Although meat and milk may not be mixed, *parve* food may be eaten with either. Jewish kitchens should have three sets of cooking utensils, one for each food group and two sets of crockery and cutlery for daily use (as well as additional festival sets). In practice, however, most people cook *parve* food in the utensils that are correct for the other two groups.

The law regarding meat and milk requires that an interval of some hours must elapse between eating meat and following it with milk; the actual length of time depends on the local community. This time gap allows any particles or aftertaste to leave the mouth. Usually the same time gap is left between eating hard cheese (made without rennet) and following it with meat, but after other milk foods it is only necessary to wash the mouth and hands thoroughly before eating meat. Many Jews leave a gap of three hours between these foods anyway. Although fish is regarded as *parve*, it is not eaten with meat. For example, meat with a fish sauce would not be permitted.

The tradition of Jewish food that we have today is largely Eastern European – not Israeli – in origin. Many Ashkenazi (Eastern European) Jews lived in great poverty and this, combined with the climatic conditions, has given rise to eating habits based on cheap, energy-giving foods. Foods that are traditionally thought of as being Jewish, such as salt beef, cheesecake and bagels with cream cheese and smoked salmon, come from the communities in the Diaspora.

Lokshen pudding is a favorite Jewish dish. It is made from egg noodles, dried fruit, spices, eggs and margarine and is baked in the oven.

Avocado with honey sauce

This recipe is an example of a *parve* starter, where honey is combined with two of Israel's most abundant crops, grapefruits and avocados.

You will need:
1 onion, finely chopped
1 teaspoon of mustard
½ cup of honey
½ cup of lemon juice
½ cup of olive oil
4 avocados
1 large grapefruit, peeled and divided into segments

What to do:
(1) Mix together the onion, mustard, honey, lemon juice and olive oil, and chill in the refrigerator for 30 minutes. (2) Cut the avocados into wedges, about the same size as the grapefruit segments. (3) Remove the outer skins and arrange on individual plates, alternating the avocados and grapefruit. (4) Spoon the honey sauce over each portion and serve.

The principles of this cuisine among Ashkenazi Jews are, to some extent, different from those of modern trends in diet, but they are, nevertheless, part of Jewish cultural life. Perhaps because of this high intake of dietary fat and sugar, many Jews suffer from diabetes and coronary heart disease in later life.

Before the festival of Passover, all kitchen utensils have to be thoroughly cleaned to remove any trace of chametz, *or leaven. This is sometimes done by soaking the utensils in hot water.*

The following recipe for *ilana*, or yeast cake, is an example of Ashkenazi cuisine.

Ilana
(yeast cake)

You will need:
1¾ cup of plain flour
½ cup of soft margarine
½ cup of sugar
½ cup of warm milk
2 tablespoons of yeast
1 egg, beaten
2 teaspoons of sugar
a pinch of salt
½ teaspoon of vanilla, or to taste

Filling:
1 teaspoon of cinnamon
3½ oz of raisins

Glaze:
½ cup of sugar
⅓ cup of milk
1 teaspoon of sugar
½ teaspoon of vanilla

What to do:
Sift the flour into the mixing bowl, add the sugar and salt, and make a well in the middle. (1) Pour the yeast, the milk and the vanilla into the well and stir in a little of the flour. Cover and leave in a warm place to rise until it has doubled in size. (2) Add the remaining ingredients for the dough and mix, then cover and leave in a warm place to rise. Mix the ingredients for the filling together. Roll out the dough to about ⅓"–½" thick. (3) Spread the filling over the dough and roll up into a long sausage. Place the roll on a greased tin and put in the oven and bake at 375°F for 30 minutes or until golden-brown. Remove from the oven and leave to cool slightly. Cut the cake into slices. (4) Boil the glaze ingredients and pour over the slices. Leave to cool.

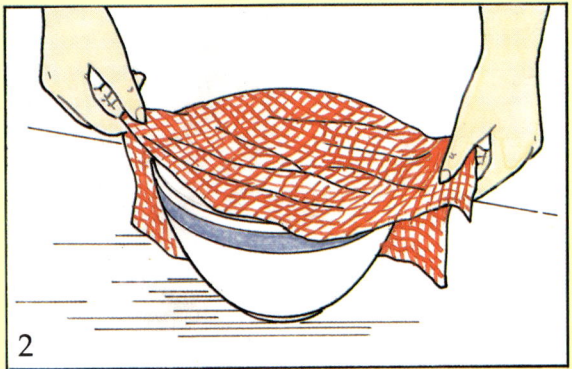

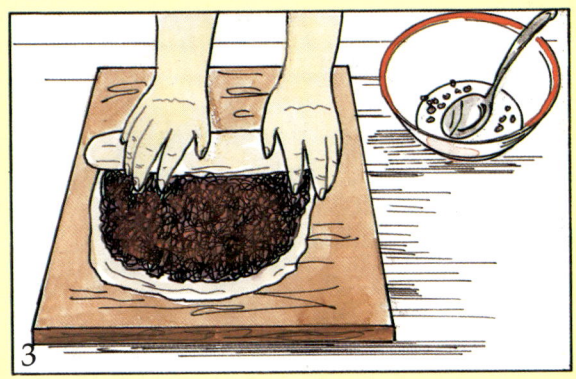

Jews of Sephardic origin have, traditionally, a lighter and healthier diet, with a greater use of fruit and vegetables. Sephardic cuisine has also been greatly influenced by the cooking traditions of Muslim neighbors. This Moroccan recipe for salad (below) is an example of the distinctive Sephardic cuisine.

The requirements of Jewish food laws have led to the development of a *kosher* cuisine. The preparation of *kosher* food outside the home, for example at butchers' shops and in restaurants, comes under the supervision of a court of rabbis known as the *Beth Din*. Food that is approved as *kosher* bears the stamp

Moroccan salad

You will need:
7 oz of carrots, scraped and chopped
¾ cup of water
1 clove of garlic, chopped
1 tablespoon of parsley
1 tablespoon of fresh coriander, chopped
2 tablespoons of cooking oil
2 tablespoons of lemon juice
1 teaspoon of salt
½ teaspoon of ground cumin
¼ teaspoon of tabasco sauce

What to do:
(1) Place the garlic, parsley, cumin, tabasco sauce and ½ a teaspoon of the salt in a grinder (or use a pestle and mortar) and make into a paste. Place the water, carrots and ½ a teaspoon of salt in the saucepan and cook for five minutes, then remove from the heat. Heat the oil in a frying pan. (2) Add the paste from the grinder and stir in half the water from the carrots. Bring to a boil, then remove from the heat and add the carrots and their remaining liquid. (3) Stir in the chopped coriander. Refrigerate before serving.

Safety note: Ask an adult to pour the boiling water from the carrots into the frying pan for you.

Above *Jews have adapted the cooking of many different countries to a* kosher *cuisine. This kosher* pizza *shop in the United States also sells the traditional Muslim dish,* falafel.

of the local *Beth Din* authority.

Because of the strict food laws, or *kashrut*, there are obvious difficulties for practicing Jews in eating outside their own homes. To a certain extent, the recent increase in the number of strict vegetarian restaurants has made it easier for practicing Jews to eat out. But in the past, eating outside the home has been limited to family meals with friends or meals served in the synagogue. The dispersal of traditional Jewish communities has meant there are now fewer small *kosher* restaurants.

However, there is a growing demand within the Jewish community for restaurants that serve *kosher* food. Therefore, a whole range of restaurants has appeared: Israeli, Chinese, Indian, Italian, all of which are *kosher* and are supervised in their food preparation by the local *Beth Din*. Obviously such a range as this is available only in the larger cities.

Left *These St. Peter fish are among the types caught by fishermen in the Sea of Galilee.*

Food production

Much of Israel's food production takes place on *kibbutzim* or *moshavim*. These two types of farming communities were created when the State of Israel was established in 1948.

Only 2 percent of the population live on *kibbutzim*, but the *kibbutz* was once central to people's ideas of Israel. Everything on the *kibbutz* is shared. Families live

Below *This picture shows a* kibbutz *in the Negev desert. Much of the land of Israel has been reclaimed from the desert by the work of kibbutzim.*

close together in bungalows, while on some *kibbutzim* children live separately in a children's house. Each person works to the best of his or her ability on the *kibbutz*, and the organization provides accommodation, food, clothing, vacation time and a small amount of money. As the *kibbutz* becomes more profitable, everyone benefits. People usually work up to eight hours a day on the land.

The *moshavim* are similar but, on

The Sharon *fruit is a variety of persimmon. It can be eaten like an apple or used like an avocado. It is in season from November to January.*

the *moshav*, families live separately. Oranges, melons, fish and chicken are just some of the products of these farms. Some of the *kibbutzim* have dairy herds and beef herds. Citrus groves are a familiar sight all over the northern half of the country.

The average annual temperature of Israel is about 20°C (68°F), but in many areas can be around 40°C (104°F). The annual rainfall varies from 80 cm (31 in) in the north to less than 10 cm (4 in) in the south.

The Jordan valley, around the Sea of Galilee, has a sub-tropical

Below *Irrigation is one of the most important aspects of food production in Israel. This irrigation machine is operated by a computer.*

Right *This area of the Jordan valley is given over to the large-scale production of date palms.*

climate. The winters can be very cold, but in March temperatures can reach up to 40°C (104°F) and the summers are extremely dry and hot. Here, where there is an adequate water supply, bananas are produced. The fruit has to be tended carefully. During the winter, each bunch of fruit has to be wrapped to protect it from the cold; in the summer the bunches are wrapped again to prevent their burning in the sun.

Avocado pears, olives, peaches and pecans are also grown. There are other uniquely Israeli types of fruit such as the *ugli*, a cross between a grapefruit and a tangerine, and *sharon* fruit, which is a type of persimmon. All the orchards have to be irrigated from March to October.

Lack of water is a great problem in Israel. When the State was established in 1948, much of the land was desert, and complex projects have been developed in order to convert land to agricultural use. The amount of irrigated farmland has increased from 75,000 acres in 1948 to 400,000 acres in the 1980s.

In the north, the Hula Valley, which was a swampy wasteland, was drained over a period of seven years and is now an area of rich farmland, which grows cotton, peanuts and melons.

Water is pumped from the Sea of Galilee down a pipeline to Tel Aviv by a system called the National Water Carrier. This forms a grid of canals and pipelines that provides water both for homes and for irrigation in the southern, drier part of the country.

The southern Negev desert was irrigated more than 2,000 years ago. Scientists have now managed to bring life back to the area by studying the water conservation techniques used then. Experiments have also been made with hydroponics. Plants are placed in gravel and water while exactly the correct amount of water and chemicals are circulated through the gravel bed. This has allowed the desert to produce vegetables and flowers at far less expense than the conventional irrigation techniques.

Agriculture is a very important part of Israeli life. The produce is essential because many neighboring states do not trade with Israel because of political reasons. However, the products (especially citrus fruits) are also important for export to other countries. With less than 10 percent of the population working in agriculture, food represents 14 percent of the total industrial production and 10 percent of total industrial exports. Agricultural exports have risen from $130 million in 1970 to over $500 million. In the same period, citrus exports have doubled, and exports of other products such as tomatoes, strawberries and melons have increased ninefold.

Processing and selling the food

Israel exports many foods to the Diaspora. In particular there are processed *kosher* foods, such as dried soups and sauces. In recent years, a large wine industry has also been set up in the area around Caesarea.

Citrus fruits are exported fresh, dried and canned. Various drinks made from them are also produced. Bananas are harvested throughout the year. When the fruit is ready to pick, the bunches are wrapped in burlap and taken to the central packing stations. Here the best fruit is selected and sent to Haifa for export. The remainder is sold in Israel. Avocado pears are also exported. Once ripe, the pears can be left on the trees for up to three months, so export orders can be filled as required.

Food is sold in many different ways in Israel. In the old city of Jersualem, for example, there are small outdoor stalls where people can haggle with the stallholder over

These Israeli oranges are on sale on a supermarket fruit counter in London.

Above *These Jews in New York City are selecting* etrogs *for the festival of Sukkot.*

Left *Bananas are an important export product of Israel. Because of the extremes of climate in the area in which they are grown, the fruit has to be wrapped in winter and summer to protect it from the weather.*

the price of the food. The large numbers of Eastern European Jews arriving in Israel at the beginning of the twentieth century led to the establishment of stores that are very similar to those they would have known at home in Poland or eastern Russia.

There are approximately half a million Arabs (Palestinians) living in the modern State of Israel. In Jerusalem, Muslim and Jewish foods are sold side-by-side in the *suq*, the Muslim market. Besides the *suq* there is the *Mahane Yehuda*, or Jewish market, with many stalls selling different types of food. The influence of immigrants from Western Europe and the United States since 1948 has led to the building of modern supermarkets in the main towns and cities.

Along the roadside there are many stands where people can stop to buy fresh fruit and vegetables, often much cheaper than they are in the cities.

In the Diaspora, the ease with which *kosher* food can be found depends on the number of Jews living in a particular area. In cities with well-established communities, such as New York, London, Sydney and Paris, it is simple to find *kosher* butchers, fishmongers and bakers, as well as grocers and delicatessens. In other areas this may well be impossible.

In recent years, there has been a general trend in eating habits toward the use of convenience foods, and this has also extended into the *kosher* food market. Many shops now stock frozen foods of traditional Jewish recipes such as *latkes* (potato pancakes – see page 42) and *blintzes* (thin pancakes filled with sweetened cream cheese).

This kosher *freezer has been cleaned free of* chametz *and contains frozen foods for Passover.*

Food and health

The centuries that many Ashkenazi Jews spent living in Eastern Europe in conditions of poverty led to a tradition of *kosher* cooking that was rich in fat and sugar to provide cheap energy. In many Diaspora countries, Jews still eat this type of food.

Recent surveys undertaken in

A healthy salad is becoming an increasingly important part of Jewish diet.

Israel show that 70 percent of the population is overweight, due in part to this traditional diet. In many Western countries there is concern about the high number of members of the Jewish community suffering from coronary heart conditions and other diet-related diseases. This has prompted many Jewish dieticians to advise parents that they should discourage their children from eating excessive amounts of fat and to turn to healthier, fiber-rich foods. They are encouraged to eat foods like *plavah*, which is an example of a fatless sponge cake traditionally made for Passover.

Plavah
(sponge cake)

You will need:
¾ cup of sugar
⅔ cup of fine *matzoh* meal (*kosher* for Passover)
2 teaspoons of lemon juice
4 eggs
a pinch of salt (*kosher* for Passover)
confectioner's sugar to dust the cake (*kosher* for Passover)

What to do:
Separate the eggs and check them for bloodspots. Place the yolks in the mixing bowl with the sugar and beat them until they have changed color to a creamy-white and the mixture is light and fluffy. (1) Add the lemon juice, the *matzoh* meal and the salt. Beat the egg whites until they are stiff and then fold them into the *matzoh* meal mixture. (2) Divide the mixture between two cake tins and put both in the oven at 350°F for 40–45 minutes or until golden brown. (3) When the cakes are cool, dust them lightly with confectioner's sugar.

Cooking Shabbat meals

Shabbat is the most important festival of the Jewish calendar and one which is celebrated fifty-two times a year.

"Six days shall work be done; but on the seventh day is a sabbath of solemn rest, a holy convocation; ye shall do no manner of work; it is a sabbath unto the LORD in all your dwellings" (Leviticus 32).

The festival, called *Shabbat* or

At the beginning of the Sabbath meal, Kiddush is said. Then the wine and bread are shared among all the people at the table while a blessing is said.

Above Gefilte *fish are a traditional part of the Friday night Sabbath meal. They are a mixture of chopped fish, onion, egg and* matzoh *meal with seasonings. They can be fried or, as in the picture, boiled.*

Left *The* challah *is a traditional braided bread, which is cut with a blessing at the beginning of the Sabbath meal.*

Sabbath, is celebrated every Friday evening by Jews all over the world.

The Sabbath is celebrated in the synagogue and in the home. No work, including cooking, is permitted on the Sabbath. The Sabbath begins eighteen minutes before sunset on Friday and ends forty-two minutes after sunset on Saturday. This ensures that no work is done on the Sabbath itself. In a real emergency, in order to save a life, for example, Sabbath rules may be lifted. Of course the time of sunset varies according to the time of year. These times are now calculated by computer and published in advance. Time may be added to the Sabbath but never subtracted.

The Sabbath meal is very important to Jewish families. It begins with a blessing, *Kiddush*, over wine, which is then shared. Next, hands are washed. Then two special braided loaves, *challot* (*challah* in the singular), are blessed and cut. These commemorate the double portion of manna (food) that the Jews received for the Sabbath while they were wandering in the wilderness. Before cutting, the loaves are covered with a cloth called a *decke*.

Because no work can be done, all the meals have to be prepared in advance. Large urns are filled with water and heated and slow-cooking food is placed in the oven in advance. Ashkenazi Jews call this type of casserole *cholent*, and

Sephardic Jews call it *adfina*. Modern ovens, with electric timers, have made this much easier.

There are many traditional foods for the Sabbath. These include such dishes as *gefilte* fish, chicken and *parve* cake.

For Saturday, the traditional food is *cholent* (or *adfina*) with *kugel* (flour and breadcrumb pudding) or rice. The following recipe for *cholent* is a traditional Ashkenazi recipe. The *kugel*, made of breadcrumbs, fat, flour and eggs, is cooked covered, in the same oven as the *cholent*. The very slow cooking turns the starch to dextrin, thus giving the *kugel* its unique flavor.

Cholent
(beef casserole)

You will need:
9 oz of dried pulses (such as white lima beans or great northern beans)
3 tablespoons of chicken fat or vegetable oil
3 onions, sliced
½ teaspoon of paprika
½ teaspoon of ground ginger
3½ lb of stewing beef
1 teaspoon of thyme
2 cloves of garlic
9 oz of pearl barley
2 lb of potatoes
salt and pepper

What to do:
Soak the pulses for at least twelve hours and then drain. Heat the fat or oil in a pan and cook the onions until soft and brown. (1) Remove the onions and add the meat, cook until brown. (2) Add all the remaining ingredients and cover with boiling water. Cover the dish tightly and bring to a boil. Put into the oven at 400°F for 30 minutes. Reduce the heat to 260°F and cook for about 24 hours. Do not open the casserole or stir it. (3) Remove from the oven when ready to eat.

Drinks

Drinks that are consumed with a meal or shortly afterward have to be chosen to match the food eaten at the meal. For example, although tea or coffee with milk may be drunk after a milk or *parve* meal, they may not be drunk after a meat meal. Many people, of course, choose to drink black coffee or coffee with a non-milk whitener in it after a meat meal. However, there is a tradition, particularly among the Ashkenazi Jews, of drinking tea without milk after meals. Russian Jews have a custom of drinking tea while holding a sugar cube between their teeth. During the festival of Passover, the same laws apply to coffee and tea as to other foods, and special products with Rabbinic seals are available.

The laws of *Kashrut* also apply to wine and wine-based spirits and fortified drinks such as brandy and sherry. This restriction was introduced because of the ancient non-Jewish practice of offering a libation to the gods. *Kosher* wine is produced, particularly in Israel, under Rabbinic supervision. It is grown, harvested, fermented and

Wine is shared out at the beginning of the Sabbath meal.

bottled by Jews. *Kosher* wine has traditionally been very sweet and alcoholic. More recently there has been an increasing trend toward growing different varieties of grapes and producing many different wines, which are now available in *kosher* stores and supermarkets.

This man is selling drinks in the streets in Israel. The drinks container strapped on his back is beautifully decorated with bells.

Festive foods

Because dietary laws are such an important part of the Jewish religion and way of life, it is not surprising that the festivals of the Jewish religious year have many special foods associated with them. In this section we shall look briefly at these festivals and the culinary celebrations associated with them.

Pesach is the feast of the Passover

These Jews in Yemen are celebrating Passover with a seder *meal. The symbolic foods of Passover are in the large basket.*

and is one of the most important festivals in the Jewish year. It is celebrated from the fifteenth to the twenty-second of the Jewish month of *Nisan* (March/April). *Pesach* celebrates the time when the Israelites escaped from slavery in Egypt. On their departure, they made offerings of lamb to God and baked *matzoh*, unleavened bread, because there was insufficient time to allow the bread to rise.

On the day before *Pesach*, therefore, all leaven is removed from the home. From now on all food that is used must be "*kosher* for Passover." Flour is not allowed, but *matzoh* meal is. This is the ground

Dairy foods such as this soft white cheese are traditionally eaten at the festival of Shavuot.

product of *matzoh*, the unleavened bread of the Passover. It is labeled "*kosher* for Passover" and is prepared under Rabbinical supervision. Not more than 18 minutes are allowed between water's being added to the flour and its being baked. This ensures that the dough does not have time to rise.

The special *seder* meal that is eaten at *Pesach* includes a lamb shankbone, a roasted egg, a spring vegetable and bitter herbs. Each of these represents some part of the Israelites' escape. There is also the sweet-tasting *charoseth*, which represents the mortar that the slaves used to build the palaces and cities in Egypt, and there are bowls of salt water that represent the tears of the Israelites.

Shavuot is celebrated on the sixth day of *Sivan* (May/June). With *Pesach* and *Sukkot*, it is one of the

Apfelküchen, *or apple strudel, is typical of the type of food made especially for the festival of* Sukkot.

three Pilgrim festivals celebrating the time when the Jews traveled to the Temple in Jerusalem. It was originally called the Festival of the Harvest, or the Day of the First Ripe Fruits. It also commemorates the time when Moses was given the Law, or *Torah*, on Mount Sinai.

It is traditional to eat dairy foods at this festival. One possible explanation given for this is that, until the Jews received the *Torah*, they were not bound by the laws of *Kashrut*. However, once they had

Left *This* sukka *has leaves and vegetables hanging from the roof. The pictures on the wall are called* Ushpizzin.

Date-and-nut pudding

You will need:
13 oz of dates, chopped
4 oz of walnuts, halved
½ cup of flour
1½ teaspoons of baking powder
½ teaspoon of salt
3 eggs
1 tablespoon of sugar

What to do:
(1) Mix together the dates, walnuts, flour, baking powder and salt. Beat the eggs and sugar together, add to the date mixture and combine well. (2) Pour the mixture into a greased 9″ × 9″ baking dish. Bake in a pre-heated oven at 325°F for 40 minutes. (3) Serve while still hot with whipped cream.

received the Law they ate dairy food until they could *kosher* their cooking pots.

The New Year festival of *Rosh Hashanah* falls on the first day of *Tishri* (September/October), and Jews hope that the New Year will be sweet and they will be blessed. Therefore no sour or sharp-tasting foods are eaten at the festival. Honey cake called *lekach* is a traditional dish for this festival.

Sukkot is celebrated from the fifteenth to the twenty-second day of the month of *Tishri*. It is called the Feast of Tabernacles. Jews build a *sukka* (shelter) in their garden to remind them of the way in which

Right *The* Chanukah *burns brightly in the window of this house.*

Below Latkes *are traditionally eaten at Chanukah. Here they are served with salt beef and pickled cucumbers.*

Potato *latkes*
(potato pancakes)

You will need:
2 large, or 4 medium-sized potatoes, peeled
1 heaping tablespoon of medium *matzoh* meal or flour
1 small onion, finely chopped
1 clove of garlic, finely chopped
1 egg
paprika
vegetable cooking oil
salt and pepper to taste

What to do:
(1) Grate the potatoes using the large-hole side of the grater. Place the potatoes, onion and garlic in a mixing bowl. Add the *matzoh* meal, salt, pepper and paprika. (2) Break the egg and check for bloodspots. If there are none present, beat it and add to the mixture. Mix thoroughly. Put the oil in a large frying pan and heat. When the oil is hot, drop the mixture into the pan, one spoonful at a time. (3) Fry until brown on one side and then turn over until both sides are cooked. Remove from the pan and place on kitchen paper to drain. (4) Serve with sour cream and/or applesauce.

Safety note: Be very careful when frying with oil.

the Israelites lived during their wanderings in the desert for nearly forty years before they returned to Canaan. All meals are eaten in the *sukka* provided that the weather is suitable. Rich, sweet food, such as *apfelküchen* and date-and-nut pudding, are typical for this festival.

The festival of *Chanukah* is celebrated from the twenty-fifth day of *Kislev* to the second day of *Tevet* (December/January). It recalls a victory that the Jews won against the Syrians in the second century BC, when the Syrians had taken Jerusalem and desecrated the Temple. When the Jews entered the Temple they found that there was only sufficient consecrated oil remaining to light the *Ner Tamid* (everlasting light) for one day, while it would take eight days to obtain more. However, the lamp continued to burn for eight days.

In Jewish homes today a nine-branched candlestick, called a *chanukah, menorah* or *chanukiyah*, is lit; one candle is lit each night for eight days until eight are burning on the last night (the ninth candle is used to light the others). Potato cakes called *latkes* are traditionally eaten during *Chanukah*, as are doughnuts.

Purim falls on the fourteenth day of *Adar* (February/March). It commemorates the story told in the Book of Esther when the wicked Haman was hanged with his ten sons after persecuting the Jews in Persia. *Purim* is a happy occasion, and a traditional food is *Hamantaschen* or "Haman's pockets," pastry cases filled with poppy seeds.

A costume party during Purim.

Appendix

There are three languages that are particularly associated with Judaism: Hebrew, Yiddish and Ladino.

Hebrew is the language of the Jewish holy scriptures and, since 1948, is now the official language of Israel.

The principal Hebrew words that you are likely to encounter in relation to food are:

challah – braided Sabbath bread
kashrut – Jewish dietary laws
kosher – permitted
shochet – ritual slaughterer
terefah – forbidden

Yiddish, a language spoken by Jews, is based on ancient German with additions from Hebrew and the Slavonic languages. Although it is spoken less these days, as more and more Jews have absorbed much of the culture of the countries in which they live, Yiddish has given many words to the English language, and particular words and phrases are often still used by Jews in the Diaspora.

Here are a few examples of Yiddish words relating to food:

bagel – ring-shaped roll
borsht – beet soup
kneidlach – *matzoh* dumplings
kreplach – type of ravioli
kugel – flour & breadcrumb pudding
lokshen – noodle
nosh – food (eaten between meals)
shmaltz – rendered poultry fat
worsht – salami

Ladino was the language of many Sephardic Jews and is a mixture of ancient Spanish and Hebrew. There are very few people who still speak it today.

Glossary

Anti-Semitism Hostility toward Jews, which may result in discrimination and persecution.
Beth Din A court of rabbis (Jewish religious leaders).
Canaan The Promised Land of the Jews.
Chanukah The Jewish Festival of Lights commemorating the re-dedication of the Temple by Judas Maccabeus in 165 BC.
Concentration camps Guarded prison camps, where millions of Jews were murdered by the Nazis

during the World War II.

Dextrin A sticky substance that is a by-product of changing starch to maltose. Dextrin is used to thicken foods.

Diabetes A disease usually caused by too much sugar in the blood.

Diaspora A term that refers to the dispersion of the Jews from Palestine after the Babylonian captivity and to the Jewish communities that arose after this dispersion.

Hydroponics A method of cultivation by growing plants in a liquid instead of soil.

Leaven Any substance, such as yeast, that produces fermentation in dough or batter and causes it to rise.

Libation A liquid, usually an alcoholic drink such as wine, offered to a god or goddess.

Parve Food that is neither milk nor meat.

Persimmon A sweet, orange-red fruit that is edible only when completely ripe.

Pesach The Festival of the Passover, which celebrates the time when the Jewish people were released from slavery in Egypt to become a free nation.

Purim The Festival of Lots, commemorating the time Esther saved the Jews from destruction by Haman.

Rabbi A religious teacher and leader and the chief official in the synagogue.

Rennet A substance, containing the enzyme rennin, which is usually made from the stomachs of calves, and is used for curdling milk in making cheese.

Rosh Hashanah The Jewish New Year festival.

Sabbath The weekly holy day.

Seder A ceremonial meal eaten in Jewish homes on the first night or first two nights of the Passover.

Shavuot The Festival of First Fruits, which also celebrates the giving of the Law and the Ten Commandments to Moses.

Shechitah Ritual slaughter.

Suq A Muslim street market.

Sukkot The Festival of Tabernacles, which commemorates the period when the Israelites lived in the wilderness.

Synagogue The Jewish place of worship and meeting.

Yahweh A Hebrew name for God.

Further Reading

Betty Crocker's Cookbook for Boys and Girls. Western Publishers, 1984

Follow the Sun: International Cookbook for Young People by Mary Deming and Joyce Haddard. Sun Scope, 1982

I am a Jew by Clive Lawton. Franklin Watts, 1985

Judaism by Myer Domnitz. Bookwright, 1986

Let's Look Up Food from Many Lands by Beverly Birch. Silver Burdett, 1985

Passport to Israel by Clive Lawton. Franklin Watts, 1988

We Live in Israel by Gemma Levine, Bookwright, 1983

Picture acknowledgments

The publishers would like to thank the following people for their permission to reproduce copyright pictures: Christine Osborne 6, 9, 11, 16, 19, 23, 24, 26, 27, 30, 31, 36, 37, 39, 40; Wayland Picture Library 17; Zefa cover, 4, 7, 13, 18, 20, 21, 25, 29, 33, 34, 35, 38, 41, 43. The artwork on page 5 is by Malcolm S. Walker. All step-by-step recipe illustrations are by Juliette Nicholson.

Index

Abraham 6, 7
Anti-Semite movements 8
Arabs 6, 25
Ashkenazi Jews 8, 10, 13, 25, 27, 31, 33
Australia 6

Babylonians 8
Bagels 10
Beth Din 15, 17
Bible 6, 9, 10
Blintzes 26

Canaan 7, 8, 43
Challot 31
Cheesecake 10
Cholent 31, 32
Concentration camps 8
Convenience foods 26
Cooking utensils 10

Dairy products 10, 39, 40
David, King 8
Diabetes 13
Diaspora 6, 8, 10, 23, 25, 27

Egypt 4, 7, 8
Europe 6, 8
England 8

Festivals
   Chanukah 43
   Pesach (Passover) 28, 33, 35, 36, 37
   Purim 43
   Rosh Hashanah 40
   Shavuot 37
   Sukkot 37, 40
Fish 2

Food Laws (*Kashrut*) 9, 10, 15, 33, 36, 37, 39
France 8

Galilee, Sea of 20, 22
Gefilte fish 32
Germany 8

Heart disease 13, 28
Hula Valley 22
Hydroponics 22

Iraq 6
Irrigation 22
Israel 4, 5, 8
   agricultural produce 18–22
   agricultural exports 22, 23
   creation of State 4, 8, 22
   Jewish population 4
   Palestinian population 25
   rainfall 20
   temperature 20, 22

Jerusalem 8, 23, 39, 43
Jews
   eating out 17
   history 6, 7, 8
   location 4, 6
   religion 9, 10
Jordan 4
Jordan Valley 20, 21
Judah 8

Kibbutzim 18, 19, 20
Kosher 9, 10, 15, 17, 23, 25, 26, 27, 33, 36, 37, 39, 40
Kugel 32

Latkes 26, 43

leaven 36
Lebanon 4
Lekach 40

Market 25
Matzoh 36–7
Meat 9, 10
Mediterranean Sea 4
Milk 10
Moses 8, 39
Moshavim 18, 19, 20
Muslims 8, 15, 25

Negev Desert 22

Palestine 8
Parve 10, 33
Passover 28, 33, 35, 36, 37
Persia 8, 43
Plavah 28
Poland 6, 25

Recipes
    avocado with honey sauce 12

cholent 32
date-and-nut pudding 39
ilana 14
latkes 26
Moroccan salad 15
plavah 28
Russia 6, 8, 25, 33

Sabbath 29, 31
Salt beef 10
Sephardic Jews 8, 15, 32
Shabbat 29, 31
Sharon fruit 22
Shechitah 10
Shellfish 10
Spain 8
Sukka 40, 43
Supermarkets 25
Syria 4, 8, 43

United States 6, 25
Ugli fruit 22

Wine industry 23, 33, 34

	DATE DUE		

641.5   Paraiso, Aviva.
PAR

              Jewish food and drink.

LONGFELLOW ELEM SCHOOL
HOUSTON TX 77025

393742 01240 50038B 00293E   04